I Dance
Dragon

Jacob Harada

*Poems of chronic illness, trauma, faith,
and reconciliation with self*

ELOQUATION BOOKS | North Vancouver

Copyright © 2024 by **Jacob Harada**

All rights reserved. No part of this publication may be reproduced, distributed, or transmitted in any form or by any means, without prior written permission.

Jacob Harada
PO Box 52214 RPO Lynnmour
North Vancouver, BC, V7J 3V5
Canada
www.jacobharada.com

Book Layout © 2017 BookDesignTemplates.com

Book Title/ Jacob Harada. -- 1st ed.
ISBN 978-1-7383057-0-4

Dedicated to my mother, Christine Harada, whom we lost too soon, but whose affection still protects and inspires me.

Contents

Acknowledgments 1
Introduction: Concerning Dragons 3
HEALING 7
Life Broke Me All the Way Open 8
Dragons 11
CHRONIC ILLNESS 13
Disability 14
Central Sensitization 16
Limp Mode 17
What Did I Miss? 19
Impaired Embodiment 23
Invisible Illness 25
Insecure 27
Pacing and Communication 29
I Am Ignited, but I Have No Power 30
The Second Arrow 35
Enough 37
Isolation 38
DEPRESSION AND SPIRITUAL SHAME . 41
Depression World 42

Choices	43
Attachment Despair	45
Panic Siege	46
The Problem	48
Shame	49
I Am Cruel	51
Wonder and Troubling Sorrow	52
If Only	54
Some Dance	55
I Saw It	56
FAITH	57
God Who Holds My Sadness	58
Bloodstream	59
Heartbeat	60
Inquisitor	61
I Choose	63
Witness	64
I Am as Much Here as There	68
And My Heart Is with You	71
I Tried	73
Not in the Running	74
So Be It!	77
Do You See the Dawn?	78
Syncopation	79

Aches Before the Bloom 83
Force Nothing... 84
You Are Living the Life.............................. 85
Affection 86
Concerning Dreams................................... 87
Exile and Wilderness................................. 90
Make It Prayer 91
STORY AND TRAUMA 95
Internecine 96
Somatic Memory.. 97
Neuro-factions... 100
We Are Chambers of Stories.................... 101
Dissonance... 102
Ransom... 103
"Home" Country 104
The Long Exhalation 108
Follow... 109
I Call You Dragon.................................... 110
Rage 111
On Burnout 113
Necessary 117
Trying to Save Everyone.......................... 118
Fall 122
I Wish 124

Falling for a Falling Star	127
I Loved Them	129
It's Been Seven Years	130
HEALING, part 2	133
A New Year	134
I Am Myself—Undivided	135
Driven	138
An Asymmetrical Parabola	143
More From Jacob	148
About the Author	149

Acknowledgments

This book emerged from healing, and my healing has depended on the support of many, particularly my father, Geff Harada, and family, who, despite adversity, have created space for me and believed in me. Nathan, Elliot, Brenna, Grace, Omi, thank you.

To my pastor Dave Sattler, who met me with compassion in vulnerable years and helped me reframe my life, thank you! I am profoundly grateful also to my counsellor, Ashley Crozier, who has guided me through trauma. Many of these poems are quite directly influenced by the healing process that your counselling has empowered me through.

I would like to warmly thank editor Christina Pfister for helping me shape this collection and thank Kaitlin Meilert for proofreading. Thank you Aleksandra Dimitrijević for the awesome cover art which so cleverly captures themes of this collection.

Thank you, Esther Doerksen, Elise Volkman, Kaleb Barkman, and Adam Wray, for thoughtfully reading and responding to the manuscript. Your impressions were invaluable.

I'm enormously grateful also to those generous backing of Sam Johnson, Adam Bodlack, Kat, Leane Winger, Shar Warkentin, Jared McDaniel, Tov Keller, Stephen Read, and Jina and Paul Lee. Thank you for helping kickstart this publication.

Finally, to my Captain through the dark, Jesus Christ, you have my gratitude and allegiance.

Introduction: Concerning Dragons

Dragons feature in a few of these poems as guardians. They present a problem in that they seem hostile—and for a time, do cause distress—but they are, by the grace of God, found to be allies in the end. The poem "Rage," for example, presents anger as a dragon. The poem validates the role of anger as a protector of one's worth. "Dragons" figures dragons as terrifying bodily experiences that I first experience only as antagonists, but which I eventually discover are messengers within my body, alerting me to damage and demanding that I attend to healing.

Some distressing bodily experiences can be understood as the body's demand for attention. Despite their function as defenders of health and safety, however, they feel like monsters in the moment.

The metaphor has helped me reconcile with myself. My embodied experience as a youth and young adult involved a debilitating allotment of depression, anxiety, chronic pain, and chronic illness. My embodied experience also involved the painful social and spiritual ramifications of these internal experiences.

One such ramification was a deep-seated belief that my body was somehow generating or indicating my disqualification from God's affection. A related ramification was the visceral sense of being unworthy of human affection and attachment. The physical and psychological storm generated by anxiety, depression, chronic pain, and chronic illness made it natural and habitual for me to perceive myself as deformed and repelling on the level of identity. On a prerational level—in the gut—I believed, "I am a monster," "I am pathetic," or "I am too heavy."

What helped me to heal was the understanding, firstly, that God loved me even as "useless" and debilitated as I was. As deep as I was in depression, God was with me—and deeper still would he go to hold me. I was not, in fact, disqualified from his affection. He saw and held even the "raw vortex" of my pain.

Secondly—returning to dragons—I was empowered to heal by being told that my bodily experiences had some truth within them to tell.

Sadness, fear, and anger were messengers. They had something to say that was true. They were largely working against me because I did not know how to hear them correctly and validate the message held in their clamour. They clamped down like the jaws of dragons because they had not been validated for a long time. They metastasized into mental illness. When I learned to hear and validate them, however, I discovered that they were telling me that I matter and that I'm worth protecting.

Similarly, the very physical sensations of chronic pain and illness were dragons, fighting for the safety and health of my body. They, too—though I initially experienced them only as threats—were agents of truth, communicating that my body and soul needed care.

This was a long journey, and it continues, but the result has been wonderful. I reconcile with myself, becoming whole.

That is why I write in the poem "I Am Myself—Undivided":

"The salvation of God
gives me back my body."

I am healing and I praise Christ, who has held the storm of me and in whom I am made whole. My body does not disqualify me from God's affection or make me unworthy of connection. I do not need to reject the parts of me I thought I had to hide or run from:

"The gospel of reconciliation
reconciles me with myself."

I've made friends with dragons. I hope that you, too, dear reader, if you find yourself fighting your own dragons, might also be given the grace to befriend them and thus reconcile with yourself.

HEALING

This whole collection of poems could be considered a testimony of how God has enabled me to heal. A few poems in particular, however, are intended to report on the story of my healing through chronic illness and trauma and present this process as a reconciliation with myself which was empowered by the patience of God. I place two such poems here at the start and the rest at the end of the book.

Life Broke Me All the Way Open

Chronic pain, bereavement, whatever . . .
depression, trauma, heartbreak,
whatever!

Life broke me all the way open,
and my soul spooled out
like chaotic loops of audiotape
wrenched out of a cassette.

I had to let it all run
and face the multidimensionality
of being human—
confront the
visceral strata
of embodiment as
a creature of dust,
and breath,
and need.

I had to face it or despair—
had to fathom bewildering spirals
of self-confrontation, repentance,
and acceptance.

While brutal and, obviously, vulnerable,
it also confronted me with the
beautiful
complexity
of being a socially situated
image of God on earth:
a bio-psycho-social-spiritual poem
fearfully fashioned in my mother's womb
and in the mind of the Creator.

My pathologies rend into me, I'm split—
fissured like a dropped vase—
but I discover in such self-confrontation
that the cracks underscore the beauty
of what God fashioned in the first place
and fashions now with the salvaged parts.

I am Kintsugi, a restored pottery.
The fissures are opportunities
for God
to be God—and create!
He runs vivid streams of gold into the
seams of me.
Thus anointed, I am held together.

My healing acquaints me with God's
playfulness
and his confounding capacity
to turn ruins into citadels—
temples that pulse with God's
generative heartbeat.
Healing *hurts*,
but mine, conducted within the incubation
of God's compassion,
has yielded a reclamation of self
and agency,
the capacity to forgive myself and others,
and my beginning to experience
life,
worship,
and mission as grace and gift
rather than crisis necessity.

Dragons

I've always loved dragons—
delighted in fantasy worlds
since I was as a child.
Dragons! Formidable objects of wonder.
They fly! They roar!
They win battles single-handedly!

I've always loved dragons,
except the ones inside me:
roaring things I caged.
I fought the monsters in me
with good Christian zeal (I thought),
until they pinned me to the earth, where—
as I lay prostrate and confounded—
God began to interpret to me
the tongues of monsters
for my comprehension.

They are but agents of truth—
offering data—
counsellors manifest in
psychosomatic webs.

They are guardians
that my dismissal made colossal
and cruel,
but whose original mandate
was to protect my body and worth.

I am not a machine.
I am a human.
I am a child.
God did not create me to squat in
the perpetual twilight of burnout,
until I die and report to Jesus
that I tried to be *useful* . . .
No. God created me to *LIVE*.

"Life," the dragon banner
they raged and I repressed
until they gave me an ultimatum
that I could not ignore,
and I was effectively
given a second chance
to choose life (over productivity)
faith (over appeasement)
and rest (as worship).

CHRONIC ILLNESS

The following poems express the experience of chronic illness and pain. Chronic pain affects one's whole life. It has influence on one's mental health and social connectedness. It causes a loss of agency and induces a "scarcity of self." Some chronic pain, like my fibromyalgia, is a "changed pain arrangement," or a reconfiguration of the nervous system due to trauma or stress. The effects on the body and mind can feel consuming.

It is my hope that these explorations might validate the distress of any reader going through something similar. I hope that, through the recognition of the weight that you carry, you will be enabled to have a little more self-compassion and be empowered to heal.

Disability

Disability
and assumptions of value that
I cannot ignore.

Applications for
concessions for some relief,
I am surviving.

Yet, I receive, as
the import of impairment,
clarification.

Drivenness, madness,
I can no longer belong
to the "hustle."

"Worthiness"—I had
assented to lies that I
had to achieve it.

Disability—
strangely a gift, even as it
arrests my striving.

I am concerned with
the moment and breathe alone—
forced into Sabbath.

Central Sensitization

Chronic stress-induced
"Central Sensitization"—
changed pain arrangement.

Life is different,
living with widespread, diffuse,
flu-like, aching sting.

Nervous system shock,
too much for too long, of course,
accumulation.

Limp Mode

My brother's car recently engaged
"limp mode,"
which, as I understand it,
is a massive limitation
of the car's function
enforced to prevent
critical damage.

That's basically what
my flare-ups are.

Due to a history
of prolonged critical burnout,
my body now switches into a
fail-safe
when passing an abnormally low
threshold of stimulus
and stress.

Like my brother's car,
whose internal computer
now imposes a speed maximum of
thirty kilometers per hour,

so now my body,
in a flare-up,
is locked to, maybe,
thirty percent capacity.

Pain, fatigue, and nausea
pin me down
and punish me severely
for pushing beyond
my imposed limits.

It's a strange way
that a compromised body
learned to protect itself.
The body has its own
"limp mode,"
which serves the function
of fail-safe.

It's exasperating.
My body no longer trusts me,
and I suppose
there are reasons
why.

What Did I Miss?

Did I miss a medication?
How am I in so much pain?
What did I do wrong?
I thought the week was going pretty well!

I suppose this is the crash
after a week of some significant exertion—
the price I pay for drawing
too hard on my resources . . .
But I thought I had been careful!

I woke up today with no capacity for humour . . .
I found it hard to smile at my father
and simply speak.

I felt like crying when I ordered a coffee
and heard my voice quiver—
again, trying to smile.
The exchange somehow
underscored how pitiful I felt.

What did I do wrong? This came on so fast.

My chest has clenched again.
It takes intention to draw a full breath.
I am grieving something,
perhaps only this present regression of health,
but I think something more—
something that I cannot identify.

This has been exasperating.

I wanted the doctors to isolate something—
pin a diagnosis to the wall—
show me charts and actionable data.

But they found nothing via blood samples
or nerve conduction studies.
I was assigned the bafflingly vague:
"Fibromyalgia," a diagnosis by exclusion.

It was embarrassing and confusing
to be as impaired as I was—
routinely flattened by the symptoms
and unable to work—
without having any medical data to "justify"
the extent of my disability.

Years passed
in which I was routinely
crushed by the pain,
completely losing momentum
on personal projects
and needing to excuse myself
from work and social opportunities.

After all the specialists
discovered dead ends—
in terms of data and intervention options—
I was sent to pain *management* classes,
which guide patients on how to
carry on with persistent pain.
I learned self-compassion,
spoon theory (pacing),
pain science, and regained
a modicum
of control over my life.

I am now better equipped
to handle these flare-ups:
emergence of pain, fatigue, and brain fog.
I accommodate them; I try not to hate them
(that makes them worse).

I am still caught off guard, however,
by this one—its intensity—
and how dramatically
it has coloured my mental health overnight.

It has run a black graphite blade sideways
over the whole canvas of my mind.

I had been feeling hopeful—strong even—
but the symptoms, in a blitz,
have staged another coup—
commandeering my body and mind.

What did I *miss*?
What did I do wrong?

Impaired Embodiment

Impaired embodiment:
the requisite—dissociation
of a crisis mind
blind to self.

Stealth sub-processes
dividing the wealth
of autonomy into
internecine monotony.

Intra-exile cast-off
colonies
forged of doleful necessity.

Operations—ceaseless—
affecting autonomic dysfunction
and disjunction of parts,
unable to validate each other,
always awake.

Hypervigilant
diligent dragon watch—sentinel
bent into form for threat ecology.

Energy—critical—burnt to preserve
the arrangement
of shards
in a pattern that functions but . . .

The self so sustained
spends so much soul
just to render in splendid futility
and land on the earth, confused.

Impaired embodiment—
a body-mind economy
irreconcilable,
requiring recalibration.
Impaired—embodiment.

Invisible Illness

I look like a healthy young
man—my pain
has no outline
when running through the scans of
modern medicine.

It's invisible—to imaging, to blood scans.
But it's *real;* I swear, it's real!
I feel it all over my body and it's *powerful!*
Or am I—crazy?
Am I just—pathetic?

I've seen so many doctors.
They measured—nothing.
"Fibromyalgia" and
"Chronic Fatigue Syndrome"
were alternately
assigned as explanations
when the scans were all normal—
a diagnosis by exclusion.

My hunt for explanations
of the syndromes is exasperating.

What even are these syndromes—really?
There are diverse
and contradictory explanations
leading me in different directions . . .
I am so—exhausted
and confused.

Central Sensitization:
explained as a change
in the pain system itself—
It's hard to validate.
It's so abstract.

The ringing ache in my limbs
blares with fury,
and the fog in my head
squats possessively,
but they don't explain themselves.
They don't send a ransom letter
and outline their demands.
They don't tell me what's *wrong*
or how—to fix it.
They just wail away
and ruin my life.

Insecure

The pain persists—for years,
I'm certain I have done so little.
I'm—ashamed.

People ask if I am working . . .
Yes. I'm doing what I can,
but my output has been such a
meager trickle.
I assume they'll think it's pathetic
unless I make it sound more impressive
than it is . . .
Then I'm ashamed of how insecure
I end up sounding.

Pain management
is my primary occupation.
I *work*—when I have strength.
I want to say:
"I haven't been successful
because I've been sick.
If I look stagnant and lazy,
that's why, dammit."
But I never say that directly.

I'm still measuring my worth
by my performance
and I'm convinced that mine
is lesser.
I'm so insecure.

Why does it matter what they think?

It's because their disapproval
would confirm what I'm
already believing in my gut:

that I'm pathetic
and left behind.

In truth, they probably don't judge me
as brutally as I judge myself.
My inner story—my cruel self-judgement—
is more distressing than the pain itself.
And, come to think of it,
it was crucifying me long before I fell ill . . .

Lord, save me from my inner voice.

Pacing and Communication

Pacing
and communication
generate safety.

I can only do what I can do
and I can tell people
what my limitations are.
I speak and am known.
I move according to
my portion.

Pace.
Measure.
Breath.
Pray.
Speak.

I can do this.
I'm not burning out this time.

I Am Ignited, but I Have No Power

I am ignited,
but I have no *power*.

I am ignited: veiled pressure,
my chest like a magma well
without a volcano
to actualize its
rage and affection.

Just a trickle of torque is
afforded my right arm engine to spin
the cable-stay cords
of Jerusalem's
bridge over the trauma gulf.

I am an architect.
I am an engineer.
I am neither.

I am exhausted—
in constant pain—
impaired and often dispirited—

driven again and again
to withdraw
when partway through
one pylon's purposing.

My momentum fails and falters.
And I'm wise enough to know now
that if I try to push through the pain
I will only make it worse.

The ache in my flesh
accelerates like a roiling hurricane—
its velocity amplified
by my neglect of its contention.
I can no longer ignore the mad
counsellor—monster—defender . . .

I begin to respond with compassion.
It is only trying to serve me—
defending my body.
I lower my expectations
for what I can accomplish in a day,
put down my tools,
and hold up my hands
in deferent surrender.

I take tentative steps,
monitoring the symptoms—
watchful as a squirrel
over the cracks in my flesh
and fissures in my soul.
I learn to be responsive
and I find a rhythm.

I waltz in gentle moderation
and dance with the dragon
supervising my probation.

Still, my ambition boils within
but must abide by the rules—
the rules of the rhythm
that manages my pain.

My zeal seeps out slowly,
perhaps like water and steam
through ground espresso . . .
compressed potential
allowed a slow, moderate vent.

Perhaps what lands in the tiny
ceramic receptacle is richer

for having been conserved
under such intense pressure—
concentrated?

I am ignited—
burning to see the world kinder
and aching to put my hands
to the raising of sanctuary—
but I am compressed.
My progress is humble.
My life must be slow.

I must surrender the dreams
that blaze in my chest
to the One from whom
I inherit all wonder and passion
and luminescent imagination.

I am, Father—
giver of every good dream—
at your disposal.

You know my capacity and purpose.
The furnace within me is yours—
as well as my very limited body.

I trust you do not resent me
for my barriers and wounds
because you do not despise
the weak and brokenhearted,
of whom I am one.

Give my burning soul its satisfaction
and heal my body, Father.
The dissonance demands an answer,
and I cannot resolve it.
You have plucked the visceral chords
at the core of my soul,
and you must produce the cadence.

I wait.

The Second Arrow

Chronic pain strikes like two arrows.

One: the pain itself.

Two: your interpretation
of the pain's impact on your identity.

Indeed, the stories you tell yourself
about what being sick
insist on your worth—
worsen the distress
when the through line is a loss
and the fixation is the cost
on the value of your life.

Let I tell you definitively, please:

You are no less
in the eyes of the Father.
You are not diminished.
He has seated you with Christ.
Indeed, that work is finished.

Your loss of power does not mean
a loss of place or purpose.
The pain is real—and it is seen—
of course!
Even so,
your life is far from worthless.

Grieve the losses in their turn
but know they don't define you.
Grace is your inheritance.
Your long endurance, even,
finds its place within rebirth.

But in the *now*,
just know you're loved.
Your life is bound
to Him who suffers with you,
and you're found in him.
The *telos**, thus, is *good*,
and you—you are cradled.
Nothing can diminish you.

Do not curse yourself with shame.

---

an ultimate object or aim.

Enough

I am occupied terrain
remaining under imposition
of imperator dominion
—strange chronic pain
and exhaustion.
Strength I took for granted once
is now arrested by the bandit prefect
at the border.

Strength—before she reaches me—
has been taxed heavily and erratically.
I receive her as a refugee—much harrowed.
I've learned to harbour her—gently.
Give asylum—demand no results.

"As you are, dear," I say to her.
"Do only what you can.
You are not condemned
for arriving decrepit.
Forget you came to build Jerusalem.
For now, it is enough to simply breathe.
Just breathe: enough—enough."

Isolation

Protective. Guarded.
Chronic illness makes me—reclusive.
I withdraw—
my tolerance attenuated, gravely.
I have no strength.
I cannot receive you graciously,
as I might have
if I was not hurting.

In the spells of health
I've so enjoyed—the weeks or days—
when not in pain,
I have so *expanded*!
Social! Happy! Confident! Assertive!
Making plans and reaching out.
Going to parties
and *enjoying* them!

I crash back into a flare-up.
Pain all over—brain fog.
Everything gets harder.
Pressing on gains a grim colouration.
Three weeks in—I'm exhausted.

The chest tightens.
The shoulders tense and guard.
Tension—Threat—Scarcity of Self.

I miss out on so many events—
and drop out of so many commitments—
to attend to the body chaos underway.
I cancel, cancel—decline, decline.
I'm sorry that I'm so weak.
I really wanted to serve this Sunday . . .
I cannot . . .

People don't realize
how hard it is to just show up,
and how doing so absorbs
a disproportionate allotment
of my strained reservoir of strength.
I crash for days after gatherings
It takes so much out of me
to play social.
I *want* to be present
but pain makes it toilsome
to get there.

I want to come to your party,
but fatigue is crushing me.
Thinking about going out today
gives me panic attacks.

In contrast,
in the spells of health I have so enjoyed,
I have discovered that I connect with ease.
Relationships feel *playful*,
I feel generous—empowered.
my capacity to connect gives me dignity.

When I return, however,
to the lonely rigor
of pain-management mode,
the social rhythms
that were giving me joy
and a sense of belonging
become inaccessible.

Sometimes the hardest part
of carrying chronic pain . . .
is the isolation.

DEPRESSION AND SPIRITUAL SHAME

The following poems express my experience of depression, anxiety and shame. They voice some despair, but they also represent attempts to catch glimmers of light while sojourning in the dark.

Depression, I think, is in part a visceral search for meaning. When distress has persisted for some time, meaning—a reliable metanarrative—is harder to hold onto. There arrives an experience of senselessness, absurdity, and detachment.

My depression was associated with spiritual shame, and a fundamental sense of not qualifying for God's affection, despite believing the right things cognitively. These poems wrestle with the fear and distress of this aspect of my mental illness.

Depression World

A little like the Upside Down
of Stranger Things,
Depression World
is a parallel dimension
with all the same geography and
city planning
but lavishly overlaid with
suffocating dusk and ashes.
Depression World is a filter veiling
even one's most intimate kinships.
They are present
but they appear convincingly
warped and aloof.

Depression World occludes
the scanning eye
to people's affection.
Loved ones who might actually care—
in Depression World they
have fangs and wings and judgement
and they do not really see you.
No one really sees you,
in Depression World.
You are an aching wraith
in a circus of monsters.

Choices

A constellation of concerns under my
sternum,
I'm wishing I had made some better
choices in my youth.

This ensemble cries a crisis—
wreaking
havoc on my notion
of what is the truer truth.

Did I miss the boat already
or am I still on the path?
Disoriented, I cannot tell
if I'm even moving in the right direction . . .

Am I caught in the critical interim,
gestation?
I'm waiting for a shipment of meaning,
to honour the radical
child-fool-warrior
who wanted to join the dance
he saw the shadows of
on the hill.

44

My chest aches from body stress
and cataclysmic mental digressions alike,
and I'm not sure that living openly
was worth it,
considering where it landed me now.

I chose to live in mission—
took the banner I saw my parents take
at their cost . . . and mine.
In duty, I opened my heart to the world,
and the world destroyed me.

There was too much pain,
and I had no barrier.
I thought the Christian heart
had to be absolutely permeable,
but my attempt to live that out
was as landing on a javelin point
and sliding all the way down.

Either I did something catastrophically
wrong
or God is not kind—
or neither, and I will yet have the meaning
assigned to my devastation.

Attachment Despair

We are jagged-edged fragments
of a broken humanity
thrust against one another
by the force of deficits.

You give your whole self
to fashion an attachment
only to find your noblest efforts
are full of need
and make you, at best,
an inconvenience,
and at worst, a threat.

Too crude and wounded,
we recoil from one another—
we who each
only want to be known.

Can anyone, ever, reach you?
Can the hidden heartache self
ever be found?

Panic Siege

Here am I again,
compressed
under fathoms of murky terror—
its constituents phasing in
and out of my compromised vision,
flashing barbed judgements.

My body is remembering
half-year long sieges of panic
in which even breathing is challenging
but a pathogenic voltage
in my nervous system
still commands me to climb.

I cannot sleep.

Two AM sprints on the boulevard,
in the harrowing mist of
spiritual anemia.

I'm running, despite the
kickbacks on my health
because it is a greater distress
to lie still
and marinate
in the fire.

I'm shouting into
apathetic concrete
which seems, like my
thought if Father
to resent the weight
and sound of me,
telling me by its silence
that I am too heavy.

I cannot sleep.

I have lost the face of God.
I can only see a distortion.
Recitations of Psalms strain
to form a bridge
but the structure seems to collapse
over this chasm.
Worship music hurts me,
with its profession of triumph
that feels facetious on my lips
and seems to confirm my
exclusion.

I am consoled only by
"Feel the Night,"
by Strahan and
"Psalm 13 (How Long O Lord),"
by Brian Doerksen.

The Problem

Perhaps the most fundamental problem
of my faith life remains the belief
in my bones
that the shame that
consumed me in my youth
was the voice and expectation of God.

It told me that I would only qualify
for consolation by being better than I was.
I believed in grace and mercy as concepts
but the theory did not take my grief
and shame away.

"Justification" was "by grace through faith"
but *comfort* had to be earned
and I had not done so, yet.

In this malignant frame—
as far as it still commands me—
God always seems to require more.
I have never done enough to qualify
for the visibility of my need
to the Father.

There is no "enough" for me and
I cannot rest.

Shame

I have shame—
I have shame in my chest
It's like walking on a broken leg—
like pushing through a barbed wire fence
with bleeding hands.

It's like the rot in the walls
of the shack we forgot—
like the wound from the rifle
shot that cracked
at the crumbling of my childhood peace in
deference to threat.

Like a toxin in the air I breathe—
a plague that seems to feed despair,
which wipes the beauty out of life
and poisons every smile.

Like critics spewing caustic noise—
an ever-present voice accusing
all my motions, all my choices,
everything I do.

Like war confined inside my mind—
an enmity that binds two sides
and never ceases to replace contentment
with distress.

I have shame—
I have shame in my chest
It's like walking on a broken leg—
like pushing through a barbed wire fence
with bleeding hands.

I Am Cruel

How the hell do I forgive myself?

My whole policy toward myself
is punishing.

An unkind word has
calcified inside
and become my spine,
defining my expression
in the world.

Hard, impatient, and resentful—
I am cruel . . .
but God is not.

"Remember me according to
your kindness, Lord,
and teach me scripts of space
and generosity.
Give me something to answer
the gut belief
that I am just a problem
that has no solution."

Wonder and Troubling Sorrow

Everyone is beautiful—vulnerable.
Wonder and troubling sorrow . . .

I'm stricken with—humility.
Who am I to judge anyone—ever?
Everything is grace.
I feel it again—it's all grace!
All I want to do right now
is show everyone how
beautiful they are . . .

But I'm also heartbroken
by the weight of our collective
being and striving and fighting and forcing

so much futility . . .

I feel again what overtook me
in that month,
when I held my dying mother's hand
and knew with transcendent assurance—
assurance that overcame
my vain obsessions—

that her life
was confoundingly beautiful
and that *life*
is an immeasurable gift.

All my striving for worth was vain—
My judgments and comparisons—
futility.
I knew it then.
I know it now.

Start now—start from here!
Love now—love now!

I am, at once, so free and so heavy.
I'm reverent and grateful
and besieged with sorrow.

If Only

Let me fall right through hell into the void
if only
there, you'll sing into my bones again
your consuming claim on me
and tell me that I'll *heal*.

Tell me you're holding me, please—
now, while I cannot see the light.
Bring me word in the dark
of the coming of your promise
and set a stage-mark for me
in the theatre of
reconciled earth and sky.

Let my sojourn in this anchorless night
run its course—
if only
here, you tell me that I'm not forgotten
and show me where next
to place my feet
and lean my heart.

Some Dance

What is my small life
and its unsated ache
against the wonder of existence?

The created order is
a breaking forth of abundance . . .
some *dance*,
choreographed in cosmic orbits
and every living breath.
It means something.
It *means* something.

I see the outline of an Artist;
I see a Dancer who delights.
I will hold out my ache to Him
and beg for metamorphosis.

I will be given back my joy—
one day.
The dance is my inheritance.
I feel it through the grief
and wonder.

I Saw It

Wonder and light!
I saw it! Just there—just a moment.
I saw it, and the night lifted.
For just a moment,
I saw it.

This doesn't end
in the valley of the shadow
of death.
Christ is my companion here,
captaining my trespass through the dark—
he is also the prince of promise and light
that I witnessed flashes of
over the ridgeline.

I saw it!
I saw it, and for a moment,
the night lifted.

FAITH

The following poems express the faith that sustained me through suffering. Some poems also attempt to capture some critical words of affirmation that I heard from God in the depth of my distress. The companionship of Christ in my suffering got me through. Words of affection shot through the darkness and saved me. I would not have gotten through the night if the Father had not taught me compassion and given me a script from which to learn embodied grace.

God Who Holds My Sadness

God, who holds my sadness—
which from my youth
has been no small thing—
you have my allegiance.
Take me through the haunting forest
and harrowing wilderness.
Show me how to sing in both
or how to be silent.

Yahweh, give me your confidence;
tell me the secret paths
through these perilous places
and give me what destiny
you believe best befits me—
I don't even care what it is.
Just hold me and counsel me
and lead me into your rest.

God, who holds my sadness,
I offer all of me, at once,
as best I know how.

Bloodstream

Tap my bloodstream
into yours.
Be
my crisis dialysis.
Run
the plasma through
the chambers of *your* heart
to purge
the scarcity scream
it stores in its storied
viscosity.

Heartbeat

I've fallen and
I haven't gotten back up.
By certain metrics,
I've never "bounced back."
I'm still down here,
but
when I fell,
I slipped through
the membrane between
kingdoms
and unravelled
in the Most Holy Place—
the Sanctum of Surrender
which is the Womb
of Knowing.

As, here, swathed in
amniotic mercy,
I slow my thrashing—
six years now, seven,
still slowing—
I hear a heartbeat that
doesn't rise and fall
with my anxiety but
stays
the same.

Inquisitor

I came at my web of
necessary lies
like an inquisitor.
Wielding bills of indictment,
I assaulted the accuser counsellors
presiding in my mind.

I only found, however,
that you cannot defeat
condemnation
with condemnation.

Like an angry surgeon,
I tried open-heart surgery
on myself, with a meat cleaver.

I only found
that you cannot heal violence
with violence.

I do not begin with the requisite
compassion.
I do not *have* it.
Neither do I have the *patience*,
though the work cannot be done
without it.

Dear Jesus,
I have a nascent faith
that you are kinder than I am
and that it wasn't you
that demanded
I become cruel.

In any case,
my attempts to heal have failed.
Here is the scalpel,
and the charge to restore.

Restore me.
Reunite me.
I am your disaster.
Save me,
or I am fearfully lost.

I Choose

As far as it is mine
to choose my comforter,
I choose life,
I choose breath,
I choose you.

I release the world—
unclench—collapse.
It's all I can do.
I've tried everything else.

As far as it is mine to choose—
to choose my consolation—
I choose you, Christ.
I can do nothing,
nothing now but wait . . .

How long—how long, oh Lord?
How long?

Witness

I've imploded over the café laminate,
grieving loss impending—
worse, hating my proclivities
which got me here again
about to shatter.

How grasping I have been—
gasping—risking—
pretending wisdom,
hiding writhing need, shame
and hating—hating
self and suffering.
Wretched need and foolish hope.

You touch my chest now
having knelt to meet me—
touch my chest and access
hidden history and its meaning—
previously undisclosed to me,
though truly it had ruled me
from my shadow mind.

You touch my chest and draw out,
like a coal from a furnace,
a landscape of the tribe,
the mountain of my parents' assignment—
and the wounding gravity.
You say you see me—
say you *see* me.

You're holding that raw vortex,
calmly.

You say that I don't need to hate myself;
my story is understood.
You contain it—
enfold it with compassion.

There is no need to compensate
or entertain a script of
debt or deficit
as a secret master; rather,
all is seen,
all accounted for.

There is no judgment
by the man who meets me at the well—
the cistern of my agony—
and who draws out
the reservoir's
summary
and holds it up to me.
He tells me everything I've ever done
and says he understands
and forgives!

So gentle,
such a switch of script—
a way to get out
and mighty wings to hide beneath,
while I chelate the toxic narration—seeping
from the pores of my soul
where it had formed
a provisional government of terror
and a crisis state of
self-reinforcing hell
consuming me
underneath a false reproduction
of competence and confidence.

This was hidden,
but you reveal it,
witness and disarm it.
You say the story isn't over.
I don't belong to the pain
but to an overstory
blooming on the underside
which validates the marks accrued
and folds them in
to burning—breakout light.

I Am as Much Here as There

*A creative rendering of what I comprehended my Lord
to tell me while I was flattened by years of pain.*

Jesus met me in my wilderness and said:
"Find you, your soul
in grief, detained,
far from the hilltop's reprieve.
You remain
below the ledge
the glad choir's pledge
alleges vic'try from.

"Find you, your body
broken on the trail thereto,
one arm reaching for temple rest,
one just pressed against
your chest
where mourns a song
less splendid, more distressed
than what the brothers and sisters
on the hill profess
while claiming life and hope
and breath . . .

"Then abide and just exist.
Arrest your fraught
and jealous wishes.

"Viscous is this wilderness,
and yet I am as much here as there.

"The desolations that you tread,
these sundered lands—
are holy ground.
The breadth of these,
these valleys, dread,
my temple spans and sanctifies.
I am as much here, in the ache,
as there, where it will resolve.

"Your walks with me
through blasted land
are liturgies of life.
Though guised in grief
they clothe you brightly.

"You are a song in shadowlands
of heaven, even here,
for I am as much here as there.

"The mighty hill is flattened down
and this low wasteland lifted high,
for I inhabit both the same.
Dismiss your shame,
for I am as much here with you
as there."

And My Heart Is with You

My Christ, my Captain, said to me:
"The earth gives way,
and still, my heart is with you.

"Mountains crack like glass—
the crashing down of might and monolith
all aroar around you,
and my heart is with you.

"You fall, I fall with you.
Gravity like that of a moon
breaks across your chest,
and my heart is with you.

"You weep and rage
and run and wage a thousand wars
in a moment
and now you're spent,
and still, my heart is with you."

Ever present . . .
he is steadfast.

"Does it surprise you
that I am stronger than the mountains?
Deeper than the sea I cast them into?
Wilder than leviathans frolicking there?"

I replied:
"Let the earth give way
and ocean swallow
structure melting into
flood and storm
if only, ever, you'll hold me."

He returned:
"I have and I will—forever.
My heart is with you.

"And when the tempest passes:
new horizon, wrought in the breaking—
new breath, this undying—
fresh crust of the earth delivered
in promise through fire and sea—
my heart will be with you."

I Tried

"I tried, my Lord; I couldn't help them.
I was far too weak."

To my surprise, you *hold* me . . .
understanding.
I collapse—I utterly collapse.
Permission to unload—and fall apart.

"I tried!" I sob. "I gave my utter all."

Compassion—I am not condemned.

I'm limp upon the kindness
of the ones you send to hold me:
siblings, fathers, friends,
pastors, counsellors.

I tried—you know.
You hold me.

Not in the Running

A literary apprehension of God my Father's voice within me after I appealed, in great distress, for comfort.

"You access your Belonging
by child-spirit trust—by faith
and not by things you do
in the frantic, uncertain
attempt to be useful.

"If you stand and wait
and let your terrors rush through you
and beyond you—
release those assumptions of inefficacy
and disqualification—
fears of not having done enough,
or not having done it well enough,
and of not being enough.

"Then, if you stand and listen in radical
stand-fast surrender-stillness,
if you let the frantic
impulse wildfire burn past you
and just dwell in the settled aftermath—

in the quiet, you did not think
you were allowed to enjoy—

there, left behind,
having lost your place
now in the kingdom of uncertainty
(sweet exile!),
you find the Kingdom in your chest.

"You find my affection.
I call you: 'delight of my heart.'
This is my verdict for you,
a suit of armor and a crown.

"You discover in stillness
that the things you feared disqualified you
from my affection and inclusion
have all been definitively dealt with.
This, too, (while my cross and kenosis)
is also my delight to accomplish.

"You have a new engine fire,
white like the heart of lightning
but patient as an eagle.

"You advance!
Consoled–alight–confirmed.
Your stride,
distinct from prior cadence
when you stumbled rapidly on
in the frigid assumption of insufficiency.

"Be still, at last, be still!
Everything—all that I have—is yours.
I have given you my very self;
what would I withhold from you?"

I escape the anemic worth-schemas
and obsolete value hierarchies
that fuel the hustle and war
of the world that lives in question.
Not in the running but in the waiting . . .

I let the world go, for the Kingdom
and my Father's affection,
which are not earned but *inherited*.
How great is his love?
Far more than I once understood—
but to know it now is enough.

So Be It!

If everything I've built so far
is but vain complicity in Empire
and Brand—
If I misunderstood,
and accidentally built the wrong temple—
So be it!
So be it, if only now, you show me
how to make my next step mean something
and then the step after that.
Illuminate the way, Christ.
You are the lamp, the sun, and the signal
by which I will find my way.

Let me die
and rise in you,
even at this very moment,
so that I can do nothing
but sing Heaven's welcome onto Earth
in organic faithfulness
that cannot be rushed
because the rhythm
is your breathing.

Do You See the Dawn?

"Do you see the dawn?"
asks my Captain, gesturing dawnward,
playfully.

I see it . . . I see it!
I have always seen it.
Long before it touched the horizon,
even in the thick of night,
I saw it in your eyes, my Captain.

Dawn—your voice's buoyancy,
affecting warmth and rest.
Dawn—the deathless levity
with which you face the test.
Dawn—you are a prophecy,
the dawn arrived in flesh.

I knew the Dawn in darkness.
It was psalmic, epinephrine shots—
Word over the water.
Captain—Dawn beside me—
I have always seen it.

Syncopation

Consider the withholding
of your dreams
to be but the—syncopation
of destiny.

The hits—delayed,
a subversion of expectation—
just a moment . . . of disappointment . . .

But when the shots land,
they'll be all the sweeter
for having been delivered
outside of your grid.

Let all things take the time they need
and let God surprise you.
Catch his
swing—
the delicious—
alternative.
Force not your presumptions.
Let go!
For dear life, let—go.

The song is wilder
and wider than you can conceive
and you *inhabit* it.
The steps can be learned.
The burden is light.

He's made a place for you
within the chorus,
with syncopated, liberated timing.
It's a stride decided by
the passion of the King—
a thing inherited
and viral like—yeast in dough
transforming and enriching.

The destinies delivered in the meter
of the Great Orchestrator
thwart our human schemas,
and circumvent our social grids.

The syncopated flavours of the
Kingdom of the Lamb
confound like crucifixion unto resurrection
(talk about subversion of expectation!).

The Risen King's *Euchatastroph-ic* cadences
season reality like salt and light.

And at the end of ends,
one chord,
"deeper than the Abyss
[and] higher than the firmament"*
will give answer to every consonance
and dissonance,
and it will absolutely satisfy and consume.

Do you know the sound of it?
The playful themes of Yahweh
writing stories,
unexpectedly,
on the underside of history.
The *slaves* are the inheritors
the *exiles* are the ones who *know,*
that even should the earth give way,
tectonic plates accede to sea's tumult—
All is not lost.
You—have not been forgotten.
The Lamb has overcome it all—and smiles.

From J.R.R. Tolkien's *The Silmarillion*, in the chapter titled, "Music of the Ainur."

Your disappointment
over your world collapsing
is understandable.
But isn't your heart now tuned
a little better
to the song that plays over all others—
the one that will outlast them?

Consider the withholding
of your dreams—
to be but the—syncopation
of destiny.
It's a shift of placement—
subverted arrangement—
and the steps can be learned.

When the shots land,
they'll be richer for it
and they will satisfy!

Aches Before the Bloom

Aches before the bloom—
shaking, breaking, breast of earth awaiting
wonder.
Watchers abide—these the sentinels
that weep on towers,
prophets on the streets
and waves and wires.

What is this but birth and breath
and welcome to the Landed Sun—
the Living Flame.
The world, undone and wrought again
in ever-song.
Its renaissance: a tumult, and an overturn—
an overcoming—a battle won!
The aches before the bloom,
when all, augmented, will become.
Behold the Breaker, Healer, Maker,
Author-King,
Partaker
of the aches before the bloom.

Force Nothing

Force nothing.
Forgive yourself.
Breathe deeply.
Attend to your health.

Take no step in fearful overcompensation,
compromising disintegration.

Force Nothing.
Exist.
Exult.
Delight.
Weep.
Worship.

Your faith, in breath-liturgy,
fierce like sunrise
and just as patiently rhythmic.
Love always.
Hope deeply.
Force nothing.

You Are Living the Life

I've been so sure that I did something,
somewhere,
and God left me behind . . .
But my friend, Adam, assured me:
"You are Living the Life,"
and there was Spirit in the words.

I'm already in . . . caught like a leaf
dropped into a gushing spring,
yielding hospitably—
a welcome into the great unfolding.
This is the Life—
an unthreatened fountain.
I am drenched.

The arms of Christ, the Fisherman,
reach like light untethered—
cast a net, and I am snared.
The lines fall for me
in pleasant designations.
My lot is mercy-swathed.
I am living.
I am living!

Affection

"Father, do I have your affection?"

My face is on the floor.
I am a desert antelope
panting for oasis respite.

"I treasure you, my child," he says.

I claim that.
I build my life on his delight.
I've perched on the mountain
of the favour of the Lord.
There is a room for me.
I learn to dwell—I nestle in.

"Your love is my asylum.
I'm safe at last.
My portion and my satisfaction
are secure in your affection.
I will rest under the shadow
of your mighty wings,
relieved."

Concerning Dreams

I'm thinking, through the smothering
brain fog
of how I thought my life would go:
silly meandering dreams of grandeur
but also honest, modest plans—
now demolished.
Vocation. Ministry. Impact. Romance.

My dreams! My dreams have died!
I needed them to save me—
give me a definition and worth!
I needed them to serve the Lord!
What am I now, so utterly incapable
of actualizing them?

"Beloved," says the Lord in answer,
"I'm still here.
My affection for you never hinged
on your accomplishments.
I loved you
before you *did* anything."

I am confronted.

I am offended—
still clutching at the dreams I'm losing—
or have already lost.

Diagnosis doom—"my life is over!"
If this is my lot in life—"I am diminished!"

"You are nothing of the sort,"
protests the Lover of my soul.
"Your life is sealed with mine.
I am your portion, vindication,
consolation, resurrection."

Ah! Aha!
Dreams? I was a slave to them!
But now, I have my soul.
I know I'm held!
Even in *this* condition
—useless—I am loved.

Compassion that I could not comprehend
in the ignorant pursuit of what I thought
would make me worthy—
compassion apprehends me now
and arrests my malignant momentum.

I will, at last, just rest.
This—which has found me finally—
this is what my soul so thirsted for.

I thought the advent of disability
was my *defeat*
and the death of my significance.
Not so!

"Give me new dreams, Captain,
dreams with no compulsivity or threat
in their composition—
dreams that are fueled by loyal love
and found in grace
and have no shade of scarcity to them."

This is a new life
in which I am defined
by the love of the Father
and not by how many of my plans
pan out.
Dreams? I was a slave to them!
But now, I have my soul.

Exile and Wilderness

Exile and Wilderness:
mechanisms of requisite dismantling
and critical unknowing—
sanctuaries of encounter with God,
as God really is,
and yourself,
as you really are.

Proximity to the burning bush—
to catch its ever-fire requires you
to take off your
shoes,
shames,
compulsions,
and assumptions
and share your
reservations with the Flame
who refines away illusion
and demands that you become
the child you smothered to survive.
Exile and Wilderness:
where you might
come alive.

Make It Prayer

Oh heart, oh heart!
Let it out!
Make it prayer as of David, of Jesus:
"Why have you forsaken me?!"

Give it a voice.
Make it prayer, make it grief.
Let it out!

Anger to burn down a city block—
turn it toward God—make it prayer.
Breathe it upward
like dragon fire.
Make it an offering.

Father! Witness!
Attend now
to my desolation.
Forget not your castaway child
dashed to pieces
by billows on jagged outcroppings
of granite
in sea.

Where were you?
Where were you
in the maelstrom?
I trusted you—or at least,
that shadow I knew of you.

Transpacific whiplash:
One aerial lap concurrent
with our mother's brain surgery,
depositing us in the postoperative
sur-reality where I prayed in the Spirit
despite my hollowness and terror.

Desolate interim:
I was a dutiful wraith
that drove my sister to school
and warmed many iterations of lasagna
while my father attended our mother
at the hospice.

I feebly attended to the exigencies,
swearing and stumbling and caving in—
recoiling from what I'd become
or always had been.

I had, despite my pretenses and barricades,
fallen for an artist at college
who had respectfully parried the devotion
and its weight of need.
The phantom council
resident in my chest had interpreted
the rejection to me as definitive
confirmation of worthlessness
and I had driven home
to my reeling family
with a fever-pitch curse
commanding the cycles of my mind.
I was pitiful,
I was a deficit.
I was the repellant maw of lack
and wounded craving,
and I *knew* it as the deer knows the teeth
of a wolf.

It was years before I could make
a compassionate delineation:
My fundamental *needs* were valid
(and not sinful),
but their *expression* was distorted
(and that, in part, by trauma).

Oh heart,
you had collected so much grief
already, *before* the heartbreaks
and the deaths.
And then they happened,
and you took compounding wounds.

The anger has been fighting *for* you
because you matter.
Give it a voice.
Make it prayer.
Breathe it upward
like dragon fire.
Let it out.
The Father will answer
the anger and grief
with *presence.*

He's a competent, compassionate Father
who does not despise the brokenhearted
and needy
but holds them and holds space
for all that they land in his care with,
as wretched a wreck as they might be.

STORY AND TRAUMA

In a class on chronic pain management, I was taught that chronic pain has "bio-psycho-social" dimensions. I would add "spiritual" to the term. The meaning is that biological, social, psychological, and spiritual dynamics in one's present life and in one's history affect the experience of chronic pain. Trauma is an important factor, increasing the distress of—or even causing in the first place—chronic pain.

The following poems explore the way bodies hold stories and trauma. Unresolved grief, repressed anger, and chronic stress play a role a my story, collecting until breaking point.

Internecine

Trauma turns internecine
the cycles of a body-mind
which otherwise would
spin their courses unto
functions
of life.

Bodies
work against themselves
which have shelved
affliction unresolved
in existential
infrastructure.

Somatic Memory

By somatic memory, I ever
live in the present and the past
at once.
The task is to honour the past
and disarm it,
but I tend not to be wise enough
for such finesse.
It feels in my flesh
like a doom—a resignation.
I resent it.
I fear it.

Trauma gets locked in the body—
reports on a story
that had no resolution.
Somatic memory
holding history that the mind
tried to purge—to no avail.
The body: a vessel
of narratives—
swishing around inside—
through which it interprets
the present.

I have to hold a council
with the protesting past
and ask the Lord
to attend the table.
We hear them out
and validate their protestations.
Christ presides over
the clashing cries
with strange, strange patience—
meeting their clamour
with compassion.

The memories are answered—
become chapters with a place
which, prior, stormed beyond their
slot in time,
infecting *now* with *then.*

Somatic memory demands
attendance—
and the task is far too much for me,
but Christ attends to the chaos
and reclaims me from its maw.

Whereas once, the memory
clandestinely commanded me,
now, the command is mine again—
autonomy restored to me.
Agency—sweet agency—
recovered from the tangle.
Christ has mined it
from the calcified un-history
which had seized my heart and mind.
I can *choose* again—with Spirit—
instead of just—reacting.
I have a "self" instead of a "monster."
I am whole—a union and a consonance.
The parts of me no longer in
inveterate war.

My somatic memories—
assigned their proper place—
they are released of their need
to stage a coup.
I am, within me, reconciled
by the patience
and kindness
of Jesus.

Neuro-factions

Like bickering children
dwell my neuro-factions
vying for attention and
arguing on the right use of time.

Their feuds were benign once.
I was able to advocate
between them
until someone gave them
machetes
and the arms race ramped
into industrial machinery.

Now they're entrenched.
They've cut lines
and bunkered in—
employing their artillery
with righteous ardor.

They belch fire at their
counterparts' battle lines.
They don't know
that they're on the same team.

We Are Chambers of Stories

We are chambers of stories—
receptacles of narratives
apparent in the way we resonate.

Appreciate your constitution
as a story—and a teller, both.

Arrest the tales you tell that trill of
gracelessness and scarcity.

Still yourself to hear them shriek.
Hold their bleak uncertainties
against the stories in your chest
of restfulness and destiny,
and welcome and security,
and abundance and equality.

Then ask which tales you most believe
and then ask, "Why?"

Dissonance

What a dissonance:
I am a veritable tyrant, within me,
but most people think I'm
relatively gracious
and kind.

I do not know, however,
the extent to which
I have actually loved,
or what of it was just the
performance
of my consuming need
to please.
I don't know if people
truly love me
or love the frantic actor
that my tyrant
kicks out onto the stage.

To breach the dissonance,
I must interview this tyrant
in the company of grace,
and convince him to step down.

Ransom

If you live your life
running from your wounds—
denying your body's appeal
to hear it—
you've inadvertently
allowed them to puppeteer you
from your shadow mind.

You are your story's
collateral thrall
and cannot be its master
until you can pay the ransom
in grief and recognition—
the tax of rehabilitation
into contentment
and compassion.

"Home" Country

One missionary kid's repatriation battle.

Cross cultural fakery:
I know some of the notes
of this social system
but I still don't know
the *key*.

I didn't grow up here.
I don't know why image
matters so much,
or how to secure it.
I don't know how to attain
inclusion.

There is no manual,
but I feel like there's a myriad of things
I'm supposed to know already.
The script is invisible,
but essential for social validation.

Ostracization
is always a possibility
here, as it is everywhere.

I'm fumbling the social cues
by which I might secure
a little belonging.

At the same time, though,
I feel like I'm losing
so much of myself
by trying to assimilate.

I wish I could share
what I've lived through
abroad,
but locals have not context
and no interest.

Ah! There is injustice here too,
and pretentious in-groups.

Ah! There is hostility
and scarcity of grace.
Ah! Money?

I didn't learn how
to parry the threats
of this land.
I learned different system
of defense on the mission field.

Here, I'm vulnerable
and confused.

The local church, even,
is such a bizarre sub-culture to me.
It was supposed to be home,
but I feel alien in its throng.

I'm still just wanting
someone to hear my aching story.

I was wounded in the Philippines,
but I also loved it, and so much
of the crazy life we lived.

Bits of my heart are scattered
across Luzon between
Baguio and Manila.
A portion lies bleeding
into Bolo's clay
and another spills into the Pacific
on a Mindoro beach.

I have to store that life
and its cry to be seen
in a vacuum sealed pack, though,
for now.

I'm thoroughly engaged,
for the present,
in learning the nebulous key
of Canada.

I must fake my way
into belonging, here.
I have to try to make
this place "home".

The Long Exhalation

Great swathes of living,
all in frantic resonance,
compound in flesh memory—
felt in found breath when
finally, screams
gushing latent in the oasis
away from dragons without.

Then, the dragons within
insist on a frenzied
annunciation of grievance—
a dialogue resolved
with patient attendance—
a protracted accounting of marks.

Free the whole story
in a long exhalation—
the pre-requisite expulsion
of dissonance
making a way in the wilderness
for a deep
breath
in.

Follow

Follow your broken heart where it,
bleeding, leads.
Follow the fissure-vented evidence—
a keloid trail, half hiding
but inviting investigation.

Follow your aching heart where it arches.
Start feeling out the line
strung through vaulted darkness.

Will I, by happenstance,
encounter a ranger
to mark out danger? Offer a candle?
God, I need fog lights, not a candle!
I need ERTs and CPR!
Here, where something festers.
I need intervention—
an intravenous Holy Word
of consolation.

I am thrashing. I am locked in place.
Paralyzed anger,
static and serrated.

I Call You Dragon

They made no place for you—
called you indulgence.
I call you dragon,
I call you war—
war for the body
besieged by expedience,
war for the soul
that was lost in the fray.

Warrior-defender,
a name and a body
and honour to blaze for —
to cry out in rage for.
A dragon ignited
for bastions, turrets, and towers
to burn.

Burn dragon.
Burn passion.
Burn champion friend
who wars in alliance with dignity lost
and fights for a soul
till the end.

Rage

I am so "nice" and so "good."
They cannot see it: my anger! I hide it.

I am a caretaker—peacemaker.
Rage!

They say I bring peace wherever I go:
a "calming presence."
They need me to de-escalate—
I am in the middle, a buffer—
I never "react" like they do;
I am calm—I am level.

They don't realize
I take all their reactive out-lashings
into my body—I *absorb* them!
I generate external peace
at the cost of the peace of my soul . . .
And now there's a firestorm
within me as a liquid flame in my chest,
down my arms.
Now it's a skein in my soul
and a thunder I must smother.

Such rage—they don't know.
I suppose I have hidden it well,
but I wish they would see.
I am sweet to them—lovely.
To *myself*—I'm a monster!

I've been holding it down in anxiety,
with nets and blocks of concrete—
whatever I can scavenge in the rubble—
to prevent its emergence
I've been terrified and greatly ashamed,
for so long,

of my rage.

On Burnout

A woman in my small group burns out
in ministry.
She quits—good for her!
She protects her health; it is necessary.

"I'm excited to get back to being *me*,"
she says . . .
I'm struck—I'm confused.

I have also just burned out and withdrawn,
but I'm certain I have no "me"
to get back to.
I have no pre-burnout iteration
that wasn't already starving to *find* itself.

No, rather, my burnout highlights
the mechanisms I have been employing
since my youth to *fabricate* "me."

The burn, for me,
began in my *parents'* ministry.

Earnest church planters
sent to one village in the Philippines.
Their feet were surely beautiful,
but they were stressed as infantry
and unprepared—
for the stuff that went down . . .

I was a child waging war in his mind
on the serenely folding slopes of
Kayapa.

The tribe, Bolo, was so beautiful,
the whole thing could have been a vacation,
if not for the disasters, dysfunctions,
the compounding of grief without redress,
mental illness, and the settling in of
condemnation in my deeper heart.

A child, offering earnestly—and hurting.
Locked-in grief—and so much shame.

Dire-tone mission calcifying in my bones,
I assumed a damaging kind of
responsibility.

I soaked in the stress
and committed like a soldier
to never burden my parents with my pain.
(The accusers within me crucified me
when I thought that I had.)

There was too much at stake—
human souls, namely—
and also my worth.
I could not afford to express
my depression, shame, or anger; rather,
I had to man my post
in mission.

Ministry burnout began in my child-mind
and commandeered my psyche
until in my twenties, when I utterly
shattered.
Twice.

I learned grace from the consequences.
I learned breath and self-compassion.
I learned to forgive my father
and the Church.

I learned the difference between excusing
and truly forgiving—
the latter acknowledges the cost.

I interrogated the narrative
I implicitly absorbed
in the duty drive.

I admitted misapprehension
while also understanding
how I came to such
catastrophically wrong
conclusions
and why I made such
commanding, visceral vows
and why I could not speak them.

The curse compelling me
was not the yoke of Christ
but a harrowing counterfeit
born of crisis intensity,
and my eldest-child sense of responsibility,
and my empathic sensitivity,
and my secret need to be
seen.

Necessary

A lie that commanded me for a score.

If God is like his missionaries—
his hands and feet—
then he is exasperated and burnt out
and though he loves his children,
he cannot afford to treat them as such
because the work is too dire.
He must wield them as machines
for the function of mission.
Their bodies must be shell casings for
the black powder of service and
evangelism.
It is necessary.

The children must bite down
on the pain
and serve
or leave the faith
or stride the sick middle
of presenting usefulness
while employing an addiction
to answer the pain.
It is necessary.

Trying to Save Everyone

Trying to save everyone
is a trauma response, I think.

It's as if some insidious javelin
punctured the membrane
of my selfhood
and now I am everyone.

More precisely, I am all the wounded
and needy.
The membrane between me
and the hurting world
is porous.

I nose dive into the gravity
of those that others reject
because I feel their loud deficits
as symphonies
tangling with my own dis-harmony.
I have a radar;
I feel ache in the room
even without a sightline.
An inner law,

like gravity,
compels me.
The application of boundaries
that everyone tells me
is so necessary and normal
feels to me like cutting off
one of my limbs.

The anxiety that saying "no" induces
is greater than the distress
of letting myself be consumed
by people's trauma-shaped
attachment compulsions.
Someone needs to save them!
(Someone needs to save me.)

Ironically, my effort to save
the outcast
only ends up hurting us both.
I am no messiah.
I am, myself, a black hole
of need;
I just make it look like
generosity.

I posture myself as a willing giver
until I am in such terror
of the way I think
they need me—
that I finally cut them off,
and the severance is tactless—
ragged.

They are confounded and angry
because I had tacitly told them
I would be there for them.
Then, I am consumed with guilt—
guilt for abandoning them
and guilt for letting myself
be so unsustainably
depended on
in the first place.

Then, I feel betrayed
because I thought that
God told me to offer myself
to the needy.

My trauma response
has Christian justification.

I feel like a hero
until I feel like a monster.

Where the *heaven* was the surge
of Spirit power that I needed
to love the hurting person
in the way that they needed?

It didn't come,
and I just hurt us both.

Trying to save everyone
is a trauma response
by which I forfeit my dignity
and emotional safety
in kamikaze dives
into other people's pain
and then feel abandoned
by God
and ashamed.

Fall

Invest your heart, boy, in a dream.
Esteem an image—a vision—
an elegant light—the sweetest frame—
a colour of choice—a voice—a name.

Found your worth, fool, in a chase,
an aspiration—a wait—a mission.

Notice, dear heart, when it crumbles,
that your humbled state
is worse off than before
you wrapped your future in
the dream of a girl's affection
and in the *presentation* of integration.
You've been falling apart the whole time,
and she could not have saved you
—she told you as much—
nor could you have saved yourself.

Fall! Fall on Jesus,
like you never have before!
Pretend no claim to competence
or to having anything at all figured out.

Start from zero absolute:
an infant in the arms of Christ,
wailing.

He can hold you.
He can hold it all.

Lose the world and your illusions.
Fall. Fall. Fall into Christ
like you never
have before.

I Wish

I wish I didn't go back to school
after that Christmas break,
when my mom was withering.

She had asked me to stay
with her.

I left
to the futility
of a crucifying semester
that I didn't even complete.
I came home halfway through
and did have some blessed time
before she died.

I performed hymns at her memorial
as my soul broke.

Also, I wish I had reached out—
followed through
on that coffee with Kilby . . .

He was found in his truck.
I was told it was either
a suicide
or an overdose.

I had helped him write poetry!
He had come so far . . .
We had been brothers.
He was such a story of victory
until he was overtaken
by his trauma ghosts, again.

I could have reconnected,
but I was so infernally busy,
trying to serve God,
secure my value
and please people.

I performed hymns at his funeral
as my soul broke
a second time.

I grieve.
I didn't know how to discern
what really mattered to me.

I didn't know how to arrest
the momentum
of my compulsion
to achieve and appease
and qualify.

I didn't know how to *stop*.

I missed moments
to just be *with*
the ones I would lose.

Falling for a Falling Star

I sat with starlight
under starlight—
the light next to me warmer,
kinder, brighter.

My heart, still chilled from frost past
not so distantly,
warmed now—
thrilled by her attentive care . . .
I willed her to stay a while
and leaned in closer.

Too close,
for this candle's tour here was temporary.
She would soon see the stars from Europe
and I still from the West.

Yet helplessly arrested were my eyes
by hers.
Her eyes,
which at times looked deeply into me
and at times looked distantly past me
to the shores of the Baltic Sea.

Ancestrally, I have roots there
but no connection now—
and what claim do I have
on its radiant new occupant
who occupied three weeks of my summer
before the predetermined shift
eclipsed the moment of collision?

It was like falling for a falling star—
a shot of bright delight . . .
then the sky was unglamorous again.

I, too, am a comet with my own gravity.
I caught her in
my orbit—for a moment,
just a moment.

Then the sky was as it was before I met her.
It's only a vacuum now,
where her light had been—
where I had leaned my heart for a moment.

I stagger.

I Loved Them

I loved them.
God bless the reckless idealists—
wounded and beautiful.
I was among them,
and we fell apart.

I loved them.

It's Been Seven Years

Mom was like a layer of atmosphere—
or the sea.
We absolutely swam in her affection,
and we did not know what we had until
she was en-withered
and the arm she held up for us faltered.
The shield that her presence
formed over us
dimmed and fizzled,
and the dark things at the edge
were able to press in uninhibited.

I strangely struggle
to remember her sometimes.
I think it's a grief response—
an instinctive withdrawal from tenderness
to save myself from pain.

But I remember warmth—
enwrapping affection and delight:
hers and mine, hers in me—
in what she permitted me
to be proud of.

I remember warmth
ambient and hug-like,
in addition to actual hugs.

Under her overwatch,
I felt life like an adventure
a little more often,
but without her delighted eyes over me,
this pilgrimage is harrowing.

I've reeled from the shock,
at least up to the present.
I see my short breaths
in the chill air of her absence—
colder–starker–sharper.

The soul is left lonely,
orphaned by the bereavement
and left to twilight
and the triage ward of God
who I'm finding
is a competent companion
but who does not take away the pain.

The Son to the Father
says himself:
"Why have you forsaken me?"

Do we perhaps share the experience
of abandonment by a parent
who didn't actually abandon us
but whose affection is nonetheless
masked by some imposed distance . . .
that distance being death and dying?

The sky goes dark,
and a membrane tears inside—
top to bottom—jagged lines.
The innermost place, exposed.

I miss you.
I wish I could see your face more clearly in
my memory.
I want to love like you did.
Well done.
Well done.
I miss you.

HEALING, part 2

A New Year

A new year:
somehow now I'm
settled.
Settled in transience—
established
in the wilderness.

I willed relief.
I gained it not by
seizing,
as I once thought I had to.
I gained it not in
taking
but in
breathing
and other disciplines
of gratitude.

I behold the dawn.
My chest unclenches, slowly.
I exhale.

I Am Myself—Undivided

I am myself—undivided.
My body is not a menace to myself
or a problem to God.
It is a temple:
a God-sanctioned space.

The physical isn't the enemy.
God is not a gnostic.
God is creator-redeemer
and lover of what he has made.

My body is not a liability.
Insistence on such was caustic to my soul.

No, I am sealed.
The price has been paid for my total inclusion,
the body not barred.
As far as I believed
that God resented my body
for its limitations of capacity,
I believed a distortion
and in a *smaller* God than he actually is.

What I performed in the assumption
of the Father's exasperated disappointment
was not worship
but appeasement.

God is not a gnostic.
He does not save
by extracting his breath from the body
as though yanking a gold tooth
from an otherwise
useless corpse—expendable.
No, God saves by breathing *again*
in these somatic vessels—
the breath placing heaven
in bodies
which now will inherit eternity
and live out eternity *now*.
I believe in resurrection, not extraction.

The salvation of God
gives me *back* my body.

The gospel of reconciliation
reconciles me with myself.

Fractal factions within me—
the grace of the Father
returns to their form.
The glue in the seams of my pieces
is the blood of the Lamb.

Reconciled with myself,
I am postured to offer
the meta-reunion,
unfolding on earth
an embodied
Alleluia.

Driven

I've been driven by two missions
all my life.

One: to serve God.
Two: to become important.

The two have been problematically,
unhealthily combined.
The second has poisoned the first,
cancerously.

Healing into integrity
has been to disarm and deactivate
the second drive
with the affirmation that
I am *already* important
and that I cannot and *must* not
live my life in an attempt
to *become* so.

I am already important:
I am visible, known, valued, loved—
enjoyed, even—by God my Father.

When my soul did not believe this,
the second drive hijacked
all the resources of my being
in its attempt to earn my value.

I felt like an anxious squatter in
God's perpetual toleration
and thus, an exile—
everywhere.

I was a resented guest
in my own life,
soldiering under the iron light
of God's exasperated
disappointment.

Getting to heaven
would be its own hell
if it was just a perpetuation
of "tolerated" but not "wanted."

It was thus necessary
to *become* worthy of his affection.
That tended to mean
being useful or effective somehow,

or being very behaved,
or being beholden
to the needs of the world
like a wind sock to the storms—
storms I was not ready for.

This is why it was said of me
that I was interminably *nice*
but also strangely *intense*.

I had to be perfectly *good*.
My people-pleasing
and spiritual perfectionism
were prisons I needed.

I pleased and performed in a fervor
to validate my existence
and justify my breath
and the space I took up in the cosmos.

I was always starting from a negative.
I assumed deficit—always.

My drivenness, then,
despite having Christian shape

and earning me awards
and people's admiration—
my drivenness for God
was not authentic worship
because it was survival,
inherently self-interested
and restless.

I'm recovering, however,
and God is reconfiguring
my drivenness.

In my reading of Scripture,
listening prayer,
and a gentle, authentic
experience of community,
I have apprehended God
say to me persistently:

"Let me love you.
Let me tell you who you are.
Let me give you your value."

And as far as I have been able to
let him do so,

I have let the second drivenness—
to become important—
dissolve.

When I do, the first drivenness—
to serve God—
softens,
gears down
several thousand notches.

I *start* from important,
valued,
beloved,
and live *from* it.

I lose the fearful drive
of deficit
and gain the gentle drive
of gratitude.

An Asymmetrical Parabola

I plummet sharply down one side—
an Icarus messiah—
a codependence martyr
in a burn-out blaze all the way down
that keeps a few people warm
and impresses a few others
who misconstrue the
reckless expenditure
of my soul for
virtue and power.

They don't know that it's
desperate.
It's a veritable cry for help
that, unfortunately,
looks like zealous excellence.

The pattern is killing me.

My soul shatters twice.
Abyssal senselessness
swallows my perception.

The arc is brutal.
Down, cruel—precipitous.
Down.

(If you've been there, I'm glad you're alive.
I'm glad you exist.)

Jesus meets me in my murky deep
(where can I go to escape him?)
and tells me exactly that:

"I'm glad you exist.
I love you.
I witness your affliction.
I am with you."

The witness and *with*-ness of Christ
become the banner of my recovery
and the anthem of my
reclamation of worth:

"I met God in the deep,
and he assured me that
deeper still would he go
to claim me and hold me."

I learn to worship
in the act of breathing.
I learn to worship
by simply healing.

I feel permitted—commissioned even—
to "be the beloved"
and represent the kindness of God,
not by anxiety-fueled usefulness
but by child-like reception of
generously supplied
belonging.

I'm enough and am counted worthy
of the Father's resilient affection,
not by qualifying myself
by my desperate zeal
but by trusting in
what's simply given.
It's grace.

Up, I slowly begin to ascend.
Up.
This side of the parabola shallow,
gradual.

Relearning existence,
beginning to truly assume
the abundance of God's affection
and feeling it emphatically
affirmed in his solidarity
with my suffering.

I abide in the witness
and with-ness of Christ.

I bear the marks of my dual collapse
and the stress of my youth,
but the marks don't *own* my story
because I belong
to Christ's affection
and to his resurrection.

Up—the way is made possible.
Up—above the waterline.
Up—healing,
still painfully slow
but saturated with meaning.

I still ache for the world
but now I'm shielded.

I don't need to let it consume me.
I have a perimeter—boundaries—
because I have worth.

My conception of mission
changes into that of an opportunity for
participation
in the inevitable exultation of Jesus.

Jesus Christ answers the groaning
around me, accosting the deep—
indwelling the great ache—
rising from it with marks—
but overcoming.

I simply need to follow the renegade Lamb
and love, according to my portion.
Living is a gift.
Living isn't killing me this time.

By grace, I have a small part to play
in the installation of the garden city.
I have the simple, though challenging,
commission to love
and it is pleasing to inhabit.

More From Jacob

Find more from Jacob Harada at his website:
www.jacobharada.com

Join the mailing list for reflections and updates on Jacob's writing and music:

About the Author

Jacob Harada lives in North Vancouver, Canada, where he writes music and poetry and feels deep feelings. He hopes, through sound and lyric, to contend for (self and social) trauma-aware compassion in the ecology of Christian thought.

Milton Keynes UK
Ingram Content Group UK Ltd.
UKHW020256021124
450424UK00013B/1064